NORM...

D0149168

VOLUME II

HOW TO MANAGE

CONFLICT

IN THE

CHURCH

CONFLICT INTERVENTIONS & RESOURCES

HOW TO MANAGE CONFLICT IN THE CHURCH:
Conflict Interventions and Resources

Copyright © 1983 by
Norman Shawchuck, Ph.D

Printed in the United States of America
Fourth Printing 1996

Published by:

SPIRITUAL GROWTH RESOURCES®
Telephone: 1•800•359•7363

ISBN 0-938180-11-8

INTERVENTIONS & RESOURCES CONTENTS

THE PRAYER OF BELIEF: A LITURGICAL CREED

We believe that where people are gathered together in love
    God is present
        and good things happen
            and life is full.

We believe that we are immersed in mystery
    that our lives are more than they seem
        that we belong to each other
            and to a universe of great creative energies
                whose source and destiny is God.

We believe that God is after us
    that he is calling to us
        from the depth of human life.

We believe that God has risked himself
    and become man in Jesus.

In and with Jesus we believe that each of us
    is situated in the love of God
        and the pattern of our life
            will be the pattern of Jesus—
                through death to resurrection.

We believe that the Spirit of Peace
    is present with us, the Church,
        as we gather to celebrate
            our common existence,
            the resurrection of Jesus,
            and the fidelity of God.

And most deeply we believe that in our struggle to love
    we incarnate God in the world.
        And so aware of mystery and wonder,
            caught in friendship and laughter
                we become speechless before the joy in our hearts
                and celebrate the sacredness of life
                in the Eucharist.

From *The Hour of the Unexpected* by John Shea.
© 1977 Argus Communications, a division of DLM, Inc.,
Allen, TX 75002. Used with permission.

SECTION I
Essential Conditions for Successful Conflict Intervention

The methods and behaviors a church utilizes to resolve conflict is perhaps its most honest message regarding what it actually believes about truth, love and justice. You will learn more about what a church believes by observing how it behaves in conflict than you will by reading its doctrinal statement.

And so it is with church leaders — their core values and "true colors" come out in the pressure cooker of conflict!

THE CYCLICAL NATURE OF DESTRUCTIVE CONFLICT

All destructive conflict behavior tends to be cyclical in nature. Persons and organizations tend to form habits of self-defeating, destructive behavior; and like all bad habits, once formed the persons become more-or-less blind to their own destructive behavior. They tend to do it over and over again, until the destructive behaviors become predictable to the skillful observer. Once the cycle is identified, one can predict within certain limits who will be doing what next.

CONFLICT INTERVENTION

An intervention is a concrete plan for breaking into the cycle, to stop the destructive behavior and to turn the person's energy and behavior into cycles of more constructive, self-enhancing behavior.

We sometimes succeed in changing behavior by accident—a word spoken at the right time, an act done without prior thought, but an intervention is a well thought out plan of concrete steps and predicted results.

All of the materials in this manual deal with interventions; not accidents that happen to have happy results.

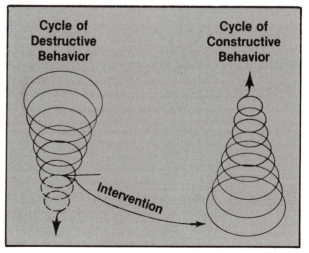

Intervention

BASIC CONDITIONS NECESSARY FOR SUCCESSFUL CONFLICT INTERVENTION

Conflict interventions may take many forms and utilize a variety of approaches and tools. Whatever the approach taken, the intervention must foster a certain set of essential conditions for bringing the conflict parties to the place where they are willing to work together to break the destructive behaviors in their relationship.

A successful conflict intervention must:

A. Help Persons Develop Their Own Personal, Psychological Power-base.

A person who is insecure or threatened in a given relationship or situation cannot think creatively about ways to resolve the conflict. A person who feels "weak" or "trapped" can think only of survival. The choice is only "should I surrender or fight?" Successful intervention, however, depends upon all persons asking, "how can I help generate the information we all need to solve this problem?"

The first consideration in conflict intervention must therefore be, "does this party feel secure enough within him/herself, and the situation, to fully participate in generating information, collaborating on solutions and entering into covenants?" If not, your first requirement is to help all the parties gain a sufficient psychic power base on which to stand in relation to the conflict.

This means you may need to strengthen your opponents in conflict. It depends on what you want. If you want to destroy your opponents, keep them weak. But if you want to turn the conflict to positive results, you must share your personal power so that in this situation all persons stand on equal psychological footing.

The question you need to ask is, "how can I help these persons feel better about themselves, to feel they are full participants in defining the conflict issues and reaching a solution?" There is no one way to do this, but once you have asked the question you are on your way.

B. Develop a Relational Base

An essential step to constructive conflict management is building a relationship of acceptance and trust. When the trust level is

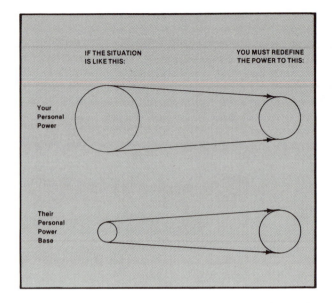

high. Almost any effort to communicate is successful. When the trust level is low, communication tends to get distorted and misunderstood.

It is, of course, better to work on issues of trust and acceptance before conflict issues arise. However, essential levels of trust can be created even in the midst of conflict if valid information is provided, and persons know free and informed choice will be allowed.

C. Establish Constructive Communications.

All constructive conflict management depends on healthy communications. Whenever conflict arises communications tend to break down—and whenever communications break down, conflict gets worse.

A primary objective in any conflict intervention must be to re-establish communications between the conflict parties. The exact process you will use to re-establish constructive communication will depend upon the particular situation.

D. Filter the Assumptions, Rumors and Charges.

A vital aspect of generating valid and useful information is to flush out all of the assumptions, rumors and charges surrounding the conflict—and to separate fact from fic-

6

tion, truth from error. It is at this point reality begins to be focused on the inevitable fears, judgmental feelings, and negative assumptions persons bring to the conflict.

Until these assumptions are identified and tested to see whether they are valid or invalid, persons will tend to fear, and believe the worst. Communicating valid information to all parties will begin moving all sides toward reality and increased trust.

E. Establish Joint Collaboration for Problem Solving and Decision Making.

The information gathering and filtering process will identify the areas of agreement and of disagreement, and begin to move the parties away from a "fight" relationship toward a "working together" relationship. Conflict divides the people over issues. Problem solving draws them together around a common task.

Identifying the areas of agreement brings immediate hope, releases energy for searching ways to cooperate around these areas of agreement, and makes the areas of disagreement seem less threatening.

The key to this step is in the turning of attention away from the causes of the conflict (since these will hardly ever be agreed upon) to what it is that the parties are trying to accomplish in the situation. You must generate a broad enough description of the parties' sincere interests and goals to be able to establish an "overlap" of agreement. Then enable the parties to work together in the "overlap." This is a crucial part of conflict management.

As persons work together in the areas of "overlap" to explore creative approaches to reach goals, greater levels of trust and communication are established. And it is in this new found trust and communiction that parties face areas of disagreement, and to work together to find creative approaches for supporting one another in the midst of their differences.

F. Establish a Covenant

After the problem solving/decision making is completed, it is vital that a covenant between the parties is established to carry out the agreements. At the simplest level this may mean rehearsing the agreements, verbally or written, allowing each party to pledge their commitment to carry them out.

In the case of more complex agreements, the covenant may contain specific times, events, responsibilities, with a "check up" plan to see how well the agreements are working, and to make necessary adjustments to avoid conflict erupting once again.

CONCLUSION

These are the necessary conditions for successful conflict intervention. When these conditions are met you will break the cycle of destructive conflicts and you will enhance the results of positive conflicts.

These conditions should become a check list against which you measure the approach you take to manage a conflict. When you are able to identify how your plan will concretely work to achieve each condition, you can be confident of having an intervention plan that will work.

The next section presents a variety of conflict interventions to guide you in planning your approaches to managing conflict. You will see that my interventions are all designed to achieve the essential conditions discussed here.

One final word before you begin your study of the intervention designs: Einstein once said, "A thing should be made as simple as possible — but no simpler."

I have tried to make the interventions as simple as possible — but no simpler. Understanding and using the designs won't be as simple as falling off a log. I am confident, however, that if you study them carefully, you will be able to adapt them to your own conflict situations. The designs are not intended for casual reading. They are tools to be picked up and used when you need them.

SECTION II

Designs for Effective Conflict Intervention

Effective conflict management depends not upon magic or mystery. What is required is a plan of intervention developed to meet the unique conflict situation—and a facilitator with the courage to stick with the plan once begun.

Before beginning a conflict intervention be sure you have a plan you trust—then stick with it.

INTRODUCTION TO THE CONFLICT DESIGNS

Following are four conflict interventions. In presenting these models, I hope to give you insight into the manner in which you must vary your conflict management approach according to the unique characteristics of a particular conflict situation. The characteristics I consider when preparing an intervention design are:

1. The size of the group involved in the conflict.

2. Whether the conflict is within one group (intragroup) or between two groups (intergroup).

3. The condition of communications and the degree of trust between the conflict parties.

4. The "stage" of conflict, according to the conflict cycle.[1]

5. The issue over which the persons are in conflict; values or traditions, goals or purposes, or policies or methods.

6. Other unique characteristics which will effect the intervention process.

These interventions are presented under the assumption you have already read the companion volume to this manual, *Volume I, How To Manage Conflict In The Church: Understanding and Managing Conflict*.

Review the designs in the light of all you have learned in this study. You will identify certain of my own preferences in dealing with all conflict situations. For example, my preference to turn every "conflict" situation into a problem solving" situation and to get all the persons talking together in a joint search for a solution. You will also note my preference to spread the conflict intervention over a number of sessions, with written assignments to be completed between sessions. You will note, however, there are times when I cannot follow my preferences. In conflict management ones own preferences must be made to serve the circumstances, not vice versa.

The designs presented each use a variety of approaches: written assignments, private interviews, Bible study, preaching, doing the entire process in one session, spreading it out over several weeks, etc. With each design are also listed the conditions in which the approach might be most appropriate. It is important to remember that these designs are intended as illustrations of what you might do. You must feel free to adapt them to your own unique situation.

For a definition of the Conflict Cycle, see page 36, *Volume I, How To Manage Conflict In The Church: Understanding and Managing Conflict*, Spiritual Growth Resources, 1983.

INTERVENTION DESIGN NO. 1:
A Small Group Design

BACKGROUND TO THE INTERVENTION

Some years ago I organized an alcoholism treatment center. The top level administration included eight professionals, each responsible for a certain work phase or department of the center.

The center grew very rapidly and we all were operating under tremendous pressures. Six months into the operation I was aware of mounting tensions within the staff. After about one year the "lid blew" in a staff meeting. Several persons began expressing pent up disagreements and anger, most, but not all, directed toward recent changes in my own leadership style and certain unilateral decisions I had recently implemented.

I knew something had to be done to resolve the conflict or staff effectiveness would be seriously impaired. Through consultation with two of the staff members, I prepared the following intervention to break the cycles of destructive behaviors we had fallen into as a staff. A week later I took the staff away for a two-day session. The following design is the plan we followed:

The two days together allowed the staff to work through several major areas of conflict. Not all the work was completed within the two days, but sufficient trust and communication had been established to allow the work to continue back home. We scheduled monthly "check-up" meetings during the rest of our time together. These were to identify new areas of tension as they developed and to allow us to deal with them before they reached serious proportions.

Though I initially developed this design for use with my own staff, I have since used it in other situations when I was working to help a group solve conflicts in which I was not involved.

CHARACTERISTICS WARRANTING THIS TYPE OF DESIGN:	
1. Group Size:	2-8 persons
2. "Type" of conflict:	Intra-group (staff, married couple, church leaders with pastor, etc.)
3. Condition of Communications:	At least some degree of mutual trust and willingness to communicate face-to-face.
4. "Stage" of Conflict:	Tension development, role dilemma.
5. "Dimensions" of Conflict Issues:	Goals, methods, policies.

NOTE: In all the designs which follow, the time column is only to hint at the amount of time which may be devoted to each step in a particular situation. You must adjust the times (longer or shorter) to fit your own needs.

TIME	GROUP/PERSON	ACTIVITY	PERSONAL NOTES
	SETTING THE STAGE		
9:00 AM	Total Group	DISCUSSION: Romans 12, The Motto Chapter for staff relationships.	
9:30 AM	Alone Time, in silence	PRIVATE PRAYERS: for our time together and in preparing one's self to participate.	
10:00 AM	Total Group	RE-MEMBERING: (putting the group back "together" again): Informal discussion to recall our common goal, our hopes and dreams that initially brought us together.	1. The "leader" must make certain each party has a personal power base. I did this by: a. Telling them at the beginning that regardless of the outcome, every one's job was secure. b. Telling them my input was to be viewed on par with theirs and the decisions we reached as a group would have my full support.
11:00 AM		Relax and lunch	
	A LOOK AT WHERE WE ARE NOW: GENERATING INFORMATION ABOUT OUR LIFE AND WORK TOGETHER		
12:30 PM	Alone Time	For every other person on staff, prepare written responses to the following: 1. Things (*behaviors and attitudes*) you do *too much* which frustrates my own work and make it personally less satisfying. 2. Things you *don't do enough* which frustrate my own work and make it personally less satisfying.	

TIME	GROUP/PERSON	ACTIVITY	PERSONAL NOTES
		3. Things you are *doing just right* which greatly facilitate my own work and make it more satisfying.	
2:00 PM	Total Group	Sharing our responses. Focusing on one person at a time, each member of the group will give his/her responses to the three categories.	NOTE: The person being focused upon may ask questions for clarification but opportunity for agreeing/disagreeing will be withheld until the evening session. NOTE: Each person will be given copies of all the sheets of responses prepared in regard to him/her.
4:00 PM	Alone Time	Private reflection on the feedback received, and prepare written responses to each staff member: 1. What I agree with in your feedback to me. 2. What I disagree with . . . . 3. What I am willing to change in our life and work together. 4. What I am unwilling to change, and why. 5. What I will need from you (and others) in order to make the changes. Dinner — 5:30 - 6:00 p.m.	
7:00 PM	Total Group	One person at a time will share his/her responses to the feedback received from the other staff members. General discussion of what we have heard and experienced.	
11:00 PM		Dismiss	

Second Day:

DECIDING STEPS TO IMPROVE OUR RELATIONSHIPS: ALLOWING FREE & INFORMED CHOICES REGARDING OUR FUTURE LIFE TOGETHER

TIME	GROUP/PERSON	ACTIVITY	PERSONAL NOTES
9:00 AM	Total Group	Morning Prayers and discussion of Phil. 2:1-15	
		Filtering the issues to arrive at priority listings of: 1. Total staff concerns 2. Inter-personal concerns 3. Private concerns with which persons need help.	To do this we will prepare a list for each member in relationship to every other staff member.
		Each member will present his/her list.	
11:30 AM		Identifying the concerns on "inter-personal" lists which must be dealt with before proceeding on "Total Staff" list.	
12:00		Lunch	
1:00 PM		Resolving inter-personal concerns.	Interpersonal concerns will begin being dealt with over lunch. If persons meeting to deal with inter-personal concerns want a "third party," another staff member will be assigned to facilitate their discussion.
2:30 PM	Total Group	Resolving issues on list of "total staff" concerns.	Concerns will be dealt with in order of priority as determined by group.
5:00 PM		Dinner	
6:30 PM	Total Group	Continue problem-solving discussions.	

TIME	GROUP/PERSON	ACTIVITY	PERSONAL NOTES
7:30 PM	Total Group	Deciding "next steps" to: 1. Continue process on unfinished business on all three lists. 2. Develop a follow through and check-up procedure to insure action is taken to implement plans/agreements.	
8:30 PM	Total Group	Covenant Service: Col. 3:12-17 A time to make covenants between ourselves, and with God, regarding the work of the past two days, and our future life together: 1. Silent reflection and writing of covenants. 2. Sharing our covenants. 3. Confessions: Personal and corporate. 4. The Lord's Supper. 5. The Lord's Prayer.	For prayers of confession we used (and I highly recommend to you) the Methodist Communion Liturgy.
9:30 PM		Dismiss	

INTERVENTION DESIGN NO. 2:
A Small Group Design

BACKGROUND TO THE INTERVENTION

I was invited to meet with a local church staff of four persons to discuss serious conflicts which were immobilizing the staff.

What Happened

My first session with them began with the director of religious education and the office administrator stating they had demanded this meeting because they were concerned about the conflict between the pastor and the associate, which was spilling over into all staff work and relationships. If the conflict were not resolved, they said, they were both going to leave the parish.

After a few moments of silence, the associate pastor announced he had already spoken to the denominational executive about leaving the parish. The senior pastor then said he, too, was making plans to leave.

I suggested if they all wanted to leave they should put no effort into resolving the conflict—since dissolving the staff would solve the problems of their relationships.

After a few moments of silence, I said the conflicts were probably not irresolvable and I would be willing to work with them; however, a requirement would be for each of them to contract with one not to leave the parish for at least six months, in which time they would seriously attempt to resolve the conflict, and their commitments to stay would need be in writing.

I did this to demonstrate:

1. It was their problem, and their decision — I would not make any decisions for them.
2. To inform them I did not see the situation as hopeless; however,
3. I would not waste my time working with a group that was not committed to the process.

What Happened

After some discussion, each one said they would do this. They were feeling guilty about leaving, but prior to this meeting the situation seemed so hopeless. They had, each one, decided there was no other alternative.

I then asked them to each write out their statement of commitment and to read it to the group before handing it to me.

I also requested to spend a half hour in private with each one before leaving. In the half hour sessions, I asked the persons to describe, from their own perspective, the root causes of the conflict.

I did this because:

1. I wanted to gain some perspective of the problem, and felt persons might be more honest in private.
2. I wanted to see if there was any agreement in their private perspectives of the problem.
3. I needed this information in order to plan my intervention into the conflict.

What Happened

A week later I met with them again to discuss my suggested approach for managing their conflict. The group agreed to my design. We were now ready to begin the actual work of resolving their conflicts. Following is the design I used.

CHARACTERISTICS WARRANTING THIS TYPE OF DESIGN	
1. Group Size:	2-6 (8?) persons
2. "Type" of Conflict:	Intragroup (family, staff, etc.).
3. Condition of Communications:	At least some degree of trust and ability to communicate face-to-face in a structural setting.
4. "Stage" of Conflict:	Injustice collecting, confrontation.
5. "Dimensions" of Conflict Issues:	All types.

TIME	GROUP/PERSON	ACTIVITY	PERSONAL NOTES

PHASE I: GENERATING INFORMATION REGARDING THE CONFLICT

Step 1: Identifying the Positive Characteristics of our Life and Work Together

Written preparation for Session I.

TIME	GROUP/PERSON	ACTIVITY	PERSONAL NOTES
	Alone Work	Carefully reflect on your working relationship with each member of the staff. Preparing a separate sheet for each person, write your responses to the following: 1. The things you do/don't do that make my own work and/or the ministry of the entire staff more effective and personally more satisfying. 2. Specifically why/how this makes my work/our ministry more effective and satisfying.	

Session I: Sharing the Written Materials

TIME	GROUP/PERSON	ACTIVITY	PERSONAL NOTES
(10 min.)	Total Group	Scripture Study: Phil. 4:1-9 Prayer for the success of our conflict management efforts.	These words were first written to a group in conflict - v.2. Today we will do/be as Paul instructed in v.8.
(3 hrs., 50 min.)		Considering the **"positives"** of our life and work together: 1. Focusing on one person at a time, the other staff members will report the results of the written assignments. 2. The "focal" person may ask questions for clarification, but may not disagree or discredit anything said to him/her. 3. (After everyone has reported to the "focal" person), a brief general discussion of the person's positive effects on the entire ministry of the staff, during which the "focal" person will remain silent.	The "focal" person will be given a copy of each person's written assessment of his/her positive influence upon the staff.

16

TIME	GROUP/PERSON	ACTIVITY	PERSONAL NOTES
(20 min.)		Closing Worship: Thanksgiving of our life and work together. Sacrament of the Lord's Supper.	

Step 2: Identifying the Negative Characteristics of Our Life and Work Together.

TIME	GROUP/PERSON	ACTIVITY	PERSONAL NOTES
Written preparation for Session II	Alone Work	Carefully reflect on your working relationship with each member of the staff. Preparing a separate sheet for each, write your responses to the following: 1. The things you do/don't do that make my own work, and/or the ministry of the staff, less effective and personally less satisfying. 2. Specifically, why/how this makes my work/our ministry less effective and satisfying.	
Session II: Sharing the Written Materials (One week following Session I)			
(10 min.)	Total Group	Scripture Study: Matt. 5:23, 24 and James 1:5-8. James 3:13-18	Today we will each discover areas in which we have not been totally wise. God's promise is we can ask for His help in our staff affairs. The Spirit will teach us. Telling another how his/her behavior on staff frustrates and angers us is very difficult—so we generally "bottle it up" inside until the "lid blows." Today, however, we will give feedback; straight, honest and in the "gentleness of wisdom."

TIME	GROUP/PERSON	ACTIVITY	PERSONAL NOTES
		Prayer for courage to be honest with each other, and the grace to be open to what we hear about ourselves.	
(15 min.)		General discussion about our fears and hopes as we begin this session.	
(5 hrs.)		Considering the **"negatives"** of our **life and work together.**	
		1. Focusing on one person at a time, the other staff members will report the results of the written assignment.	The "focal" person will be given a copy of each person's written assessment of his/her negative influence upon the staff.
		2. The "focal" person may ask questions for clarification, but may not disagree or discredit anything said to him/her.	
		3. (After all persons have reported to the "focal" person), a general discussion of the person's negative effects on the entire ministry of this staff, during which the "focal" person will remain silent.	
(15 min.)		General discussion about our experience during the session.	

(20 min.)		Closing Worship
		  Scripture: James 4:1-3, 6-10
		
		Prayer for wisdom as we begin searching together for ways to remove the sources.
		  Sacrament of the Lord's Supper.
			Now we know much more about the source of the quarrels and conflict among us.

18

TIME	GROUP/PERSON	ACTIVITY	PERSONAL NOTES
		PHASE II: NEGOTIATING AGREEMENTS TO STRENGTHEN THE POSITIVE AND TO REDUCE THE NEGATIVE ASPECTS OF OUR WORKING RELATIONSHIP	
Written Preparation for Session III	Alone Work	Carefully reflect on your own notes and the written reports given you by each staff member.	
		Prepare a separate report to each person, write your responses to the following:	
		1. The contradictions I see between your report and the others; characteristics you experience negatively while others experience positively.	
		2. The negative characteristics listed by you which I am willing to change: a. Those I can handle by myself, and specifically what I will do to change the situation. b. Those with which I will need help (what, who?) c. Specifically, (1) what I will do to change the situation; (2) what I want you (or others) to do to change the situation.	
		3. The negative characteristics listed by you which I will not change, and specifically, **why** it is important to me not to change.	
		4. Other characteristics about which I need more information before deciding whether to change or not; what I need to know is _____ .	

TIME	GROUP/PERSON	ACTIVITY	PERSONAL NOTES
Session III: Sharing the Written Materials			
(One week following Session II) (15 min.)	Total Group	Scripture: Acts 15:1-13, 19-22a	1. The Apostles also had great conflicts, vv.2, 7a. 2. They confronted the areas of conflict, and 3. Negotiated agreements, vv. 19-22a. NOTE: The advantage of the "Council" was that while some were carrying on debate, the others were able to objectify the information. Perhaps Paul and Barnabas might have reached agreement in their conflict had they brought it to the Council. Acts 15:36-41.
(4 hrs., 20 min.)		Prayer for the success of our negotiations today. Responding to the **"feedback"** we have received from each of the other staff members. 1. Responding to one staff member at a time, each person will report the results of the written assignment. 2. The two persons will: a. Identify areas of agreement. b. Negotiate the areas of disagreement until: 1) agreement is reached, or 2) it is clear agreement cannot be reached. 3. The conversation will continue until: a. All major issues have been negotiated and agreements reached, or	The person being responded to will be given a copy of the written report. During this process the other staff members will monitor the conversations to: 1. Be sure the persons are "hearing" each other 2. Encourage directness in conversation and open, honest display of emotions. 3. Suggest alternatives if requested. 4. An assigned person will keep written record of all agreements/decisions reached.

TIME	GROUP/PERSON	ACTIVITY	PERSONAL NOTES
(15 min.)		b. It is decided agreement is not possible, and decisions are made regarding future working relationships in the midst of the differences. General discussion of the negotiation/agreement process so far.	
(10 min.)		Closing prayer. END OF DAY I, SESSION III	
Session III, Day II			
(20 min.)	Total Group	Hymn: Guide Me, O Thou Great Jehovah Prayer for the session.	
(4 hrs.)		Reflections on yesterday's work session. Negotiation/agreement process continued until conversations are completed.	
(15 min.)		General discussion of the entire negotiation/ agreement process.	
(5 min.)		Closing Prayer	

TIME	GROUP/PERSON	ACTIVITY	PERSONAL NOTES
PHASE III: COVENANTING TOGETHER TO KEEP THE AGREEMENTS WE HAVE MADE — AND TO LIVE TOGETHER "ACROSS" THE UNRESOLVED DIFFERENCES.			
Written preparation for Session IV			
	Alone Work	Carefully reflect on the agreements/decisions you reached with each of the other staff members and write a statement to each person: 1. Of the extent to which you will commit yourself to keep the agreements/decisions; and 2. Any other personal word you want to give to the person. THEN Write a statement to the entire staff regarding the degree of your commitment to *all* agreements (and disagreements) reached by the staff.	
Session IV: Sharing the Covenants			
(5 min.)	Total Group	Prayer for success of our covenant making session.	
(1 hr.)		Making covenants with ourselves and with God regarding our future life together.	A covenant is "a very serious promise."

TIME	GROUP/PERSON	ACTIVITY	PERSONAL NOTES
		Round I	*Scheme: Round I*
		1. One person (#1) will read his/her "statement" to Person #2. Person #2 will respond with his/her statement to #1.	
		2. #1 will read statement to #3. #3 responds.	
		3. #1 will read to #4. #4 responds.	
		Round II	*Round II*
		1. #2 read statement to #3. #3 responds.	
		2. #2 read statement to #4. #4 responds.	
		Round III	*Round III*
		1. #3 read statement to #4. #4 responds.	Each person will be given a written copy of the statements written to him/her.
		Round IV	If major discrepancies or potential problem areas appear in the individual or staff statements, negotiate them before proceeding.
		Each peron will read statement written to entire staff.	
(15 min.)		Presentation of ourselves and our statements to God.	Gathering all written statements in a "mountain of commitments" on a center table, ask all persons to: 1. together lay hands on the commitments; 2. each to offer silent and/or verbal prayers for God's help to keep them.

23

TIME	GROUP/PERSON	ACTIVITY	PERSONAL NOTES
(10 min.)		Set "check-up" dates to review the commitments and to solve any problems that have arisen.	
(30 min.)		Group reflections on the entire process through which we have come.	
(15 min.)		Scripture: II Cor. 5:17-20 Sacrament of the Lord's Supper	We have reconciled ourselves to one another. God is also a member of this staff. We must also be reconciled to Him.
		CELEBRATION — of our Conflicts and our working to manage them by having dinner together at your favorite restaurant. END of Conflict Intervention.	

INTERVENTION DESIGN NO. 3
A Large Group Design

BACKGROUND TO THE INTERVENTION

I was invited to a church in which the members, sixty plus years of age, were in serious conflict with the young parents over the presence of a day care center which occupied a part of the church building and was operated by an independent agency.

The older members were insisting the center was filthy, poorly managed, a discredit to the church and should be immediately evicted from the building.

The young parent members were insisting it was the only center accessible to them for their children, and that it must stay.

The conflict had led to hostile exchanges in administrative board meetings and in a congregational meeting called to deal with the problem. The two groups were now at "logger heads." Communication had broken off.

We scheduled the meeting for a Sunday afternoon, 1:00-6:00 pm, with a lunch to be served from 12:00-1:00 pm so persons could remain at the church following the 11:00 am worship service.

I asked to preach in the worship service and used as my text, Psalm 133, "Behold how good and how pleasant it is for brothers (and sisters) to dwell together in unity . . . for there the Lord commands the blessing—life forever."

About seventy persons attended the afternoon session. I went there knowing certain important things:

1. The conflict focused on one major issue: the day care center.
2. The two sides were entrenched, communications had ceased, confrontation was inevitable.
3. Given the bitter history of the conflict, I had no assurance of ever getting the two sides together again.
4. The differing parties were, however, all members of the same church. In spite of the conflict, they were united around a core set of values and they all wanted the best for "their" church.

Given these conditions I designed an intervention to quickly generate a high degree of tension and emotional energy which I hoped to channel into an all out search for a solution. Since I was to be with them only once, and they were already at a "stand-off," I could not take a low-key approach in which the opposing groups might simply spend the time glaring at each other in stony silence.

I also reasoned that given the long standing duration and the extreme positions taken in this situation, there might be a build up of resentments and "brokenness" which would need be dealt with before the persons would be "free" to work together.

Following is the design I used to conduct the session:[1]

CHARACTERISTICS WARRANTING THIS TYPE OF DESIGN:	
1. Group Size:	20-100+ persons
2. "Type" of Conflict:	Inter- or Intra-group
3. Condition of Communications:	Little or no trust and communications have been broken.
4. "Stage" of Conflict:	Confrontation
5. "Dimensions" of Conflict Issues:	All types

---

[1] Parts of this design were suggested by Dr. Newton Malony, Fuller Theological Seminary, in a lecture, 1976.

I. Preparing for the Conflict Resolution Session(s):

A. Acknowledge the Conflict

- Name it. Own it. Do not deny or ignore it.
- Preach a sermon regarding the important place of conflict in the Lord's work.
- Visit personally with major conflict parties to affirm them and encourage them not to give up in the search for satisfactory solutions.
- Publicly announce conflict resolution sessions.
- Send personal letters of invitation to attend conflict management session(s).

II. During the Conflict Resolution Session(s):

A. Acknowledge the Conflict (5 min.)

"We are here to work together to find a solution to a serious conflict."

B. Remind Them of the Elements of the Faith That Still "Makes Them One" in Spite of the Conflict. (25 min.)

1. Remember who we are . . .

- We are all loved of God
- We are all less than perfect, in fact, we are sinful
- We are all forgiven—brothers and sisters, born of God's love
- We are each one unique, different, because God wants us to be so
- We are all Christians—followers of Christ, who have decided to live and serve together in spite of our differences.

2. Recognize the importance of differences among God's people . . .

- God calls upon each of us to make a unique personal response to His call to our lives
- The Christian faith requires an individual and unique response, as well as a group response. The uniqueness of individual responses will often cause differences and resistances as the group attempts to make its faithful response.
- Differences of opinion are not sinful. To resist another's point-of-view is not sinful
- It is sinful to resist the will and revelation of God's plan for us. It is sinful to destroy or to break relationships with a Christian brother or sister because they differ from us, or are resisting our ideas.

3. Consider the present situation

- Our individual responses to the (day care center issue) are conflictual— but this is our response, as best we know how to respond . . .
- Therefore, this conflict is not bad, but good in the eyes of God
- As God's family we honor one another's differences as each person's best effort to understand and do God's will
- Rather than weaken persons in their response to their understanding of God's will, we must strengthen them. Even while we disagree, we must empower each other to make his/her faithful response - and we must respect each other's differences. This is the way of God in conflict.

4. Consider the value of conflict

- Conflict increases motivation
- Conflict gets people's attention, and energizes them
- Conflict gets people involved, and commits them to decisions
- The value of this conflict for the day care center issue is that it has gotten all of you involved, it has energized you, it has captured your energy and your imagination - and when you finally settle your differences and find the best solution, you will all be motivated and willing to join forces in carrying it out.

C. State the Conflict Issue

Invite others to clarify any misperceptions

in the statement - and stay at it until there is vebal agreement that the issue has been clearly stated . . . then write it on a board so everyone can see it. (15 min.)

D. Escalate the Tension Level and Sense of Seriousness About the Conflict. (15 min.)

1. Separate the persons into opposing sides

   a. Divide the room with a strip of white tape on the floor.
   b. Hang two "position" posters on opposite walls, on either side of the tape.
   c. Instruct the persons to declare which side they are on, and how strongly they support that position by placing themselves on either side of the tape, as near or far from the wall as they feel will best describe their "conflict position."
   d. Instruct anyone who truly has no position on the conflict issue to join you in a neutral zone.

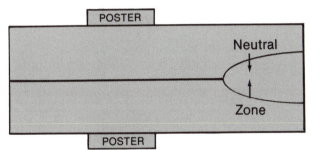

   e. When all are positioned, have them standing and facing the "other side." Instruct them to look into the faces of their opponents, observe who they are, and the extent to which each one agrees/disagrees with their own position.

   Then while they are facing those on the other side . . .

E. Encourage Each One to Reflect on His/Her Attitudes and Behaviors Toward Those on the Other Side (not toward the conflict issue), and to Seek Forgiveness and Reconciliation with Anyone with Whom Relationships have been Damaged due to Differences. (30 min.)

1. It is not a sin for us to be in conflict, but it is possible for us to act sinfully while in conflict.

   Three types of sinful attitudes/behavior which are common in conflict are:

   a. *Aggression/destroy:* "I will go through you. Annihilate you physically or psychologically; i.e., character assassination."
   b. *Manipulation/put down:* "I will go around you. I won't listen to you. You aren't important."
   c. *Separation/ignore:* "I will go away from you. I will turn my back on you. I will leave you because I don't need you."

   Each of these destroy the person or the relationship and are, therefore, sinful.

2. Urge persons to reflect on their relationships and responses to the persons on the other side - and if there is one or more against whom they have sinned in attitude or behavior, to go to those persons to ask forgiveness (not for the difference but) for that which has damaged their relationship because of the difference.

3. (When movement across the dividing line has stopped) Announce forgiveness for all sin; i.e., I John 1:9 and John 15:3.

   Then have the two groups each be seated under their "position poster" and . . .

F. Generate Understanding (not agreement) Between the Two Sides. (20 min.)

1. Sharpen the two positions by:

   a. Asking each side to prepare a brief statement outlining their position as strongly as possible: *what? why?*, etc.
   b. Have a representative from each side read their group's position statement to the other side.

2. Form dyads or quartettes comprised of persons from the two sides to discuss,

clarify and understand the other's position: (30 min.)

- "This is my position . . ."
- "This is why it is important to me..."

This is to help persons understand the other person's position.

Persons are not to argue or to try to change the other person's mind. Neither are they to defend their position by putting the other position down.

When once you think you understand the other person's position and why it is important to him/her, state it in your own words and ask if you clearly understand what he/she is saying. Keep at it until understanding is reached (not agreement).

Have the persons return to their side, under their poster . . .

G. Have each side discuss their understanding of the other side's position, and why it is important to the persons.

- What did they say . . .?
- Why is their position important to them?
- How do we feel about their perceptions? (30 min.)

H. Dialogue Together Until a Resolution is Formulated that can be supported by both sides. (40 min.)

1. Form groups (6-8 persons) representing the two positions, by combining groups from Step E.

   The groups are to:

   a. Generate possible solutions to the conflict, in keeping with the commitment to a collaborative or a support approach.
   b. Select the one alternative most strongly supported by the group.

2. Have the two sides form their groups to: (20 min.)

   a. Discuss the alternatives considered in the small groups.
   b. Decide where the group is presently in its own thinking, and prepare a resolution to suggest to the other side.
   c. Have a representative from each side announce (to the other side) where they are in their thinking and suggest any possible solution for the other group's consideration. (10 min.)

   Allow a brief time for conversation between the two representatives — for purposes of clarification only.

   d. Have the two sides continue their own discussions in the light of new information received from the other group, i.e., "How do we feel about their recommended solution? What are the strengths and/or weaknesses of the plan? How can we build on their idea?" (20 min.)
   e. Hear reports from the two representatives. (10 min.)

   NOTE: Repeat steps d. and e. until a solution is formulated which is agreeable to both sides.

   Allow 10-20 minutes for each round. Shorten the length of time in "position" group discussions as agreement grows closer and the need for communication between the two group representatives increases.

I. After Agreement is Reached

1. Remove all physical signs of the "dividedness" of the groups.

   - Pull up the dividing tape, tear up the position posters, and have the two groups move to form one group in the middle of the room. (5 min.)

2. Celebrate the ending of the conflict. (25 min.)
   a. Remind them again of the faith which has united them, and of what they have done:

- have honored the dignity of God's unique creation in each one
- have struggled, confronted, confessed, forgiven - have allowed your faith to be operative in conflict - to guide, convict, inspire
- we are none of us perfect; neither as individuals, nor as a group. Neither are we static. There will be more conflict . . .
- but God will be there leading us, forgiving us. God will help us find resolutions.
- His promise to us is, "Lo, I am with you always."

b. Celebrate the sacrament of the Lord's Supper, emphasizing the healing of all our brokenness through the brokenness of Christ's own body.

c. Serve a lunch to allow persons to relax together before leaving.

III. Following Up the Conflict Resolution Session(s):

A. Within one week, follow up the conflict session by:

- deciding "next step" plans to
- activate the agreement
- establishing "check-up" procedures and dates to monitor the plan.

CONCLUSION

In the situation in which I used this design there was considerable movement across the line as persons re-established broken relationships, see Step F.

The test of this design comes in Step H. Here the group must search for the elusive key to resolving their conflict. In our situation, the break-through came in the second round of discussion when the older group reported they had arrived at a new definition of the problem, that perhaps the younger parents were not adamant the center be in the church building - but that there must be a center within that area to which they could conveniently take their children.

The parents confirmed this to be their major concern.

The older folk then proposed that the congregation buy or lease a center facility selected by the young parents and that a center board comprised of young parents and older persons be appointed to operate the day care center or lease it to another agency; and that the center in the church building be evicted at the time the new center opened. This proposal was accepted by the young parents.

Had an agreement not been reached by 6:00 pm, I would have recommended that a task force of three persons from each side be created to formulate a resolution and present it to the total group for their consideration, within two weeks.

NOTE: I planned to do the entire design from 1:00-6:00 pm, ONLY BECAUSE NO MORE TIME WAS AVAILABLE. My preference for this design is to have an entire day, or an afternoon and evening to allow for sufficient rounds of moving from **position groups** to **representatives meeting** to assure arriving at an acceptable resolution.

With more time you might even allow the **mixed groups of eight** to meet again, after two rounds of **position groups and representative meetings**.

If after several rounds (perhaps four) it becomes obvious no progress is being made, appoint a task force, referred to above, to negotiate a resolution and report back at a later meeting.

INTERVENTION DESIGN NO. 4
A Medium or Large Group Design

For use when the group in conflict does not have final responsibility for deciding how the conflict will be resolved.

Sometimes a group will become so enmeshed in conflict they cannot, or will not resolve it, and another person or group with more authority decides something must be done; i.e., conflict in the music committee about which the administration board decides to take action, conflict in the staff about which the personnel committee decides to take action. In such instances, the higher ranking group will often ask that someone study the situation and report to them regarding steps to resolve the conflict.

In such a situation you will want to solicit the cooperation of the group in conflict in generating information about the causes of the conflict; and, if possible, in preparing a range of alternatives for resolving the problems. From this information you will prepare your own final recommendations to the committee in authority. This approach is vital in order to:

1. Generate the best information possible regarding the cause of the conflict.

2. Gain the maximum possible amount of support from the group in conflict for the recommendations you must finally make to the authority group.

When working with a group to formulate a reccommendation for resolving a conflict which must be approved by a higher ranking committee, it is important that you:

1. Never give away your responsibility for making final recommendation. The group can be fully involved but the final recommendation must be the one you think is best.

2. Never promise the group more than you can deliver.

3. You must keep your own opinions to yourself while the group is working, or some will come to understand you are not going to support their position and will give you no more information.

BACKGROUND TO THE INTERVENTION

The lay personnel committee of a local congregation requested my help to solve serious problems among its very large staff. In an exploratory meeting with the committee it became clear the congregation was in eminent danger of a split if the situation did not improve soon. I agreed to work with them, and to submit my recommendations for resolving the situation within eight weeks.

Following is a copy of the design I followed in working with the personnel committee and their staff:

CHARACTERISTICS WARRANTING THIS TYPE OF DESIGN	
1. Group Size:	15-100 persons
2. "Type" of Conflict:	Intra-group, Inter-group
3. Condition of Communications:	Little or no trust and communications have broken off
4. "Stage" of Conflict:	Injustice collecting, confrontation
5. "Dimensions" of Conflict Issues:	All types
6. Other Characteristics:	a. The group in conflict is not the final decision maker regarding the step to be taken to resolve the conflict. b. You are reporting to the final decision making group, but want the maximum amount of support possible from the group in conflict for the recommendations you will make.

PHASE I: CLARIFYING EXPECTATIONS AND RESPONSIBILITIES
(Contracting) with the Personnel Committee

MEETING WITH THE PERSONNEL COMMITTEE

1. Get their description of the conflict going on in the staff and why they feel they must intervene.

2. Clarify their expectations of myself.

3. Develop agreement:

   a. What I will do.

   b. How they will support me.

   c. The length of time I will need to do the assignment.

   d. The type of report they want/I will give.

TIME	GROUP/PERSON	ACTIVITY	PERSONAL NOTES
PHASE II: SOLICITING STAFF COOPERATION			
Meeting with Entire Staff			

1 hr.	Total Staff	1. Get acquanited
		2. Report on meeting with personnel committee.
		3. Solicit their cooperation to:
		  a. Generate valid and useful information.
		  b. Generate solutions to their problem(s).
		4. Answer any questions.
		5. Assignments in preparation for private interviews.
			Generate information through:
			1. Written materials
			2. Private interviews
			3. Staff meetings

31

TIME	GROUP/PERSON	ACTIVITY	PERSONAL NOTES
PHASE III: GENERATING INFORMATION REGARDING THE CONFLICT			
Step I: Written Preparation for Private Interviews			

	Alone Work	Write your responses to the following:
		
		1. From your point of view, what are the problems here?
		   a. General problems
		   b. Staff problems
		2. What have you done to cause the problem(s) or to aggravate the issue(s)?
		3. From your point of view, what have each of the other staff persons done to cause the problem(s) or to aggravate the issue(s)? (Write a separate response for each person.)
		4. What do each of the other staff members think you have done to aggravate the issue(s)?
		5. What are you *willing* to do to solve the problem(s)?
		6. What are you *unwilling* to do to solve the problem(s)?
		7. What would each of the other staff members say you must do to solve the problem?
		8. What do you think each of the other staff members will have to do before the problem is solved?
		9. What else do you want to tell me about the staff and the entire situation?
			Allow one-two weeks for this assignment.

Step II: Private Interview Sessions			
1-1/2 hr. each	Interviews with Members of Staff	1. Discuss his/her written materials. 2. Ask questions for additional information. 3. Answer questions.	Interviews lasted two days.

TIME	GROUP/PERSON	ACTIVITY	PERSONAL NOTES
1/2 hr. each	Interviews with members of the congregation	Interview Questions: 1. What are the strengths of the staff and congregation; what's happening that you feel good about? 2. What are the weaknesses of this staff and congregation; what's happening that you don't like? 3. What suggestions do you have for improving the functioning of the staff and/or congregation? 4. What else would you like to tell me that I haven't asked about?	Interviews lasted one day, and were arranged by the personnel committee.
Step III: Meeting with Entire Staff			
1/2 hr. each	Total Group	Bible Study: Romans 12:1-21	
	Alone Time	Reflect on the scripture and jot down your responses to the following: 1. What does this scripture tell me about God? 2. What does this scripture tell me about myself? 3. What does this scripture tell me about our life and work together as a staff?	
	Total Group	Discussion of responses to the Bible Study questions.	
2-1/2 hr.	Total Group	1. Report: "What I have learned so far about the problems confronting you as a staff." 2. Confrontation discussion of the report. 3. Assignments in preparation for next session. Dismiss	This was my report to them, based upon their written assignment and the interviews.

TIME	GROUP/PERSON	ACTIVITY	PERSONAL NOTES
PHASE IV: GENERATING ALTERNATIVES FOR RESOLVING THE CONFLICT			
Step I: Written Preparation for Next Session			
	Alone Work	Prepare a set of recommendations for resolving the conflict, and state *why* you are making these recommendations.	Allow one week for this assignment.
Step II: Staff Meeting to Search for Most Workable Solution.			
1/2 hr.	Total Group	Bible Study: Col. 3:12-17	
	Alone Time	Reflect on the scripture and jot down your responses to the following: 1. What does this scripture tell me about God? 2. What does this scripture tell me about myself? 3. What does this scripture tell me about our life and work together as a staff?	
1 hr.	Total Group	Discussion of responses to the questions. 1. Each person report recommendations for conflict resolution. 2. General discussion of the individual recommendations. 3. Identify similarities, differences. Search for "key" to resolution.	As each person reports, list the main points on a board so all can see. NOTE: If working with a large group, 1. Allow two weeks for written assignments to be mailed to you. 2. Prepare a report to the group listing the different recommendations. This will replace individual reports.
1 hr.	Small Groups	Reflecting on all the recommendations, prepare a resolution which would be most supported by all the members in your group. Lunch Break	

TIME	GROUP/PERSON	ACTIVITY	PERSONAL NOTES
1/2 hr.	Total Group	1. Hear reports from the small groups. 2. General discussion of the recommendations.	Encourage open confrontation of issues and of persons to allow all persons to speak and to discover who is supporting/not supporting their opinions.
1 hr.	Small Groups	Reflecting on all that has been said, prepare a resolution which the group feels would be most workable.	Groups to self-select around areas of agreement regarding resolution.
1/2 hr.	Total Group	1. Hear reports from small groups. 2. General discussion of the recommendations.	
1 hr.	Small Groups	Reflecting on all that has been said, revise your resolution, or prepare a new one which the group feels would be the possible solution to the problem. *and* Prepare a detailed rationale as to why you feel this is the best solution.	Allow persons to return to same group, or to join another, if they find themselves in greater agreement with it.
1/2 hr.	Total Group	1. Hear reports from small groups. 2. General discussion of the resolutions and rationales.	1. Identify points of similarity that *all* or most persons can support. 2. Identify points of differences where apparently no agreement can be reached.
1/2 hr.	Small Groups	Write a final proposal stating specific steps for resolving the conflict *and* rationale for each step.	
1/2 hr.	Total Group	1. Hear proposals. 2. Test for possible concensus, etc. Dismiss	

PHASE V: MAKING RECOMMENDATIONS TO THE PERSONNEL COMMITTEE

Step I: Preparing the Written Report:

In preparation for meeting with personnel committee, write a complete report showing:

1. The process I used.

2. The proposals, with rationale, formulated by the staff.

3. My own proposal with supporting rationale.

4. A statement of why I recommend this approach over other possible approaches.

Step II: Meeting with the Personnel Committee:

1. Present my report.

2. Allow time for general discussion, questions and answers, etc.

3. Facilitate committee decision making (accept my report, decide a new approach, etc.).

4. Decide next steps to implement approved plan.

SECTION III

Additional Readings in Church Conflict Management

READING NO. 1: A Process for Healing Broken Relationships After It's Too Late to Resolve the Conflict Issue

An Adaptation of Intervention Design No. 3, page 25

BACKGROUND TO THE INTERVENTION

Cal Bremer, a Christian Reformed pastor in Lansing, Illinois was asked by the denomination to consult with a small congregation, sixty-five members, which was slowly dying due to an unresolved conflict.

Two years previously the congregation had gotten into the conflict. After about a year of fighting the pastor left. This divided the congregation between those who wanted him to go and those who wanted him to stay.

Now, more than a year later, the congregation was paralyzed in conflict; shouting matches, name calling, members dwindling away.

Through observation and private interviews, Cal gained the following information:

1. All recent efforts to get the congregation together to discuss the issue had failed. They would only come together at Sunday worship.

2. Those who were still attending were expressing commitment to the church, but also a fear that the congregation would be "dead" within six months.

3. Chances of retaining another pastor were slim since no faction in the congregation could muster a majority vote, and voting was split along the lines of opposition.

4. The most important condition was, of course, the fact that the former pastor was gone, and he wasn't coming back.

Cal came to me with a question, "What do you do when a group is in conflict over an irreversible situation?"

"The first thing I would do," I said, "is give them valid and useful information - and you already have all the information this group needs:

1. The pastor is gone! All the fighting in the world cannot change that reality.

2. The only choice they have now is whether to mend their broken relationships and get on with the business of being the church, or continue fighting until the church dies."

"After that," I said, "I would structure an intervention in which the congregation would be thrust into a crisis moment of decision—a moment in which they would have to decide for or against a future for the church. And I would want to do this in such a way that they would feel strong commitment to their decision."

I then told Cal about my experience with the congregation that had split over the Day Car Center, see Intervention No. 3, p. 25, and gave him a copy of my intervention design saying I thought it might give him some ideas.

I'll let Cal tell you in his own words what happened next:

STEP I: PREACHING ON CONFLICT IN THE CHURCH

I arranged to preach in the church on a Sunday when the Sacrament of the Lord's Supper was to be observed. The sermon dealt with Acts 15 and was titled: "Conflict and the Church."

Introduction: Conflict in the church is much like having a sliver in your foot. You must first admit it is there before you can really decide what to do about it.

I. Conflict has Always Been a Part of the Christian Church.

   A. Galatian Church - Galatians 2

   B. Corinthian Church - I Cor. 1

   C. Philippian Church - Phil. 3

   D. Quotes from the Reformation

   E. Acts 15

      1. Council at Jerusalem
      2. Paul and Barnabas

   F. This church, today.

II. Conflict in the Church Springs From a Variety of Causes.

   A. We usually assume it is a result of "sin in the camp." This may be true, but generally sin is not the cause.

   B. The usual cause springs from individual and unique differences.

- God wants us to be unique individuals, not little tin soldiers all marching in lock step formation.
- As individuals we perceive things differently:
  - Some Jewish Christians thought the Gentile Christian should be circumcised, others saw things differently.
  - Barnabas thought Mark should go along on the missionary tour; Paul saw things differently.
  - Some of you thought Pastor Smith should stay here; others of you saw things differently.

III. Sin Does Enter Some Church Conflicts.

   A. When we use other people.

      1. As tools to be manipulated.
      2. As sand piles whom we bull-doze with no regard for feelings.

   B. When we ignore other people.

      1. Refuse to speak with them or deal with them.
      2. Reject all their ideas without consideration.

   C. When we play God.

      1. Pretend that we are the only source of truth.
      2. Pretend that we know the motives of others as if we possessed omniscience.

IV. Those Who Come to the Lord's Table Must Examine Their Own Lives and Acknowledge Their Sin.

STEP II: CALLING THE CONGREGATION TO SELF EXAMINATION AND RECONCILIATION

"Generally at this time we would use the liturgical form to engage in self-examination. This morning I would ask all of you who have been part of the conflict here or have been directly involved by the conflict to join with me in a time of congregational self examination in the fellowship hall.

We shall all celebrate together the Supper of our Lord in about fifteen minutes. Now, let us prepare ourselves for the supper in the fellowship hall." (End of sermon.)

At this point, I walked out of the sanctuary and into the Fellowship Hall. After a few moments, two or three persons stood and made their way to the fellowship hall encouraging others as they came. Soon the entire group was in the fellowship hall. I began by telling them that this session was for the purpose of seeking reconciliation so that we could sit down at the table of the

Lord as a community which was experiencing healing.

I then said, "We all know the focus of the conflict that has caused so much pain and division in this church over the past three years has been the leadership, and vision for the ministry of this church, of Pastor Smith.

Many of you have told me of your love for him as a person, but you disagreed with his style and vision for ministry. Others have told me his vision was right for this church.

All of you who were in support of Pastor Smith's style and vision, please stand over there. Those who were opposed, please stand over here. And all who were neutral, stand here."

After a few moments they began to place themselves in groups. I then asked each group to quickly write two lists: the first being a list of things which they felt others had done to them, the sins others had committed against them. The second being a list of ways in which they had been hurt by this conflict. They were informed that the lists would be read by me, I might ask questions of clarification but they would not be allowed to interrogate each other about the things which appeared on the lists.

After allowing time for the lists to be compiled I asked the groups to turn them in. First, I read the lists of sins which had been committed as perceived by each group. Secondly, I read the lists of ways in which individuals had been hurt.

After reading the lists I said, "You have now heard what your brothers and sisters think, and how they feel. Now hear the Word of the Lord from Matthew 5:24, "If you are offering your gift at the altar and there remember that your brother and sister has something against you, leave your gift there in front of the altar. First go and be reconciled to your brother; then come and offer your gift." The sacrifice of Jesus has been laid upon the altar once for all. But we profane God's gift to us if we treat it with less respect than did the people of the Old Testament.

Those who would come to the table of the Lord to celebrate Communion must be reconciled to their brothers and sisters. You have come to the table, you have had your memories refreshed that your brothers and sisters have something against you, you have heard the desire of the Lord that you be reconciled by going to your brother or sister. The time is NOW. Will you go?"

In the deafening silence, people stood fixed, staring into the eyes of others across the room. Then suddenly they were all moving to find each other and to ask forgiveness and to be reconciled.

STEP III: CELEBRATING RECONCILIATION AT THE TABLE OF THE LORD

After about ten minutes, while emotions were still high and the process was still going, I announced it was time to celebrate together the Supper. The Communion Feast was at hand.

Gradually people came into the Sanctuary where with brevity I read the simple word of the feast liturgy: "Take, eat, remember and believe, that the body of Jesus was broken for complete remission of all our sins."

Then we sang a hymn of unity and heard the benediction of peace: "Peace I leave with you. My peace I give to you . . . and now may the peace of Christ that goes beyond our understanding guard your hearts and minds . . ."

STEP IV: INFORMAL TIME TO CONTINUE THE RECONCILIATION PROCESS

Following Communion, I invited the congregation back to the fellowship hall for coffee and cookies. Everyone came—there were many intense conversations, more confessions and much reconciliation.

READING NO. 2: A Communion Service for the Church in Conflict

COME, LET US BREAK BREAD TOGETHER . . .

MOMENTS OF REFLECTION

HYMN: Holy, Holy, Holy

CELEBRANT: We present ourselves to you, Lord God, the creator of us all. We are men and women united in a common ministry and priesthood in your name, but with the limitations that only you can heal. Behold, Christ stands at the door and knocks. If anyone hears his voice and opens the door, Christ will come in and eat with them, and they with him.

CONFESSION OF SIN

Lord, we would rather be alone with you than with one another as brothers and sisters. It is so much easier to deny the humanity of those around us than it is to really share with everyone and affirm all they have to offer. We prefer to separate and be separate. We want to forget your greater demand of love. We want to keep our lives as religious people a private issue. We have sinned against our brothers and sisters and we have sinned against you. Forgive us for our lack of faith, our lack of love. Help us to be one in you, even though we are not always united in this world. Have mercy on us; forgive us our sins. Strengthen us in devotion to you and to our community in you; And through the power of the Holy Spirit keep us in everlasting life. Amen.

SCRIPTURE AND REFLECTION

Romans 12:1-5 (or John 10:11-16
Acts 2; I Cor. 12; II Cor. 3:1-3)

HYMN: Blest Be The Tie That Binds

SHARING OF THE PEACE

CELEBRANT: Jesus said: *Peace I bequeath to you, my own peace I give to you, a peace the world cannot give, this is my gift to you. Do not let your hearts be troubled or afraid.*
Let us exchange with one another the sign of peace.

CELEBRANT: May the peace of the Lord be with us all.

PARTICIPANTS: And also with you.

CELEBRANT: May Jesus' peace reign in our hearts. It is for this that we are called together as parts of one body. See how beautiful it is to dwell in unity. We who are many, are one in this bread. Lord bless this bread and wine, and bless us too, that we may celebrate this communion with joy. And so, we who have been redeemed by Christ and have been reborn by the water and the spirit bring before you these gifts. As the grain was gathered from the mountains, hills, and valleys, to become one bread, we too have come together to become a single body, the body of Christ. As too, this wine and water were mixed to become the body and blood of the new covenant, the blood Christ shed and has shared for us, Sanctify us also; change us to become your one united people to serve you as a community waiting for your reign, serving the world in your name. Lord, you have given us the world to delight in. We thank you for the things which mean so much to us.

PARTICIPANTS: The community gives thanks. Lord, you brought us into the world to help one another. We thank you for our brothers and sisters, the stars in our lives. And especially for Jesus Christ, through whose light our chains have been broken and who has joyfully joined our hands. The community gives thanks. Therefore we join our hands and voices in your praise.

O Lord, you have made us in your love, and when we had fallen and neglected you and also neglected our brothers and sisters, you in your love and mercy sent Jesus Christ, born of a woman. He shared our human nature, lived and died for us, as one of us. Through your grace Christ opened up the way of freedom and peace to us all.

CELEBRANT: For Jesus died on the cross for us all. Through his life which he gives for us, he spares us from further suffering. When the hour came he took his place at the table, and the apostles with him. And he said to them: *I have longed to eat this passover with you before I suffer; because I tell you, I shall not eat it again, it is fulfilled in the kingdom of God.*

Then, taking the cup, he gave thanks and said: Take this and share it among you, because from now on, I tell you, I shall not drink wine until the kingdom of God is fulfilled.

Then he took some bread and when he had given thanks, broke it (breaking and blessing of bread) and gave it to them, saying, *this is my body which will be given for you; do this to re-member me.* He did the same with the cup after supper, and said: *This cup is the new covenant in my blood which will be poured out for you.*

PARTICIPANTS: Therefore, O Lord, we place before you the signs of our faith, our bodies and our souls, before the eyes of all the people. We are confident that we find you in the breaking of the bread. Seal our lives in the new covenant that you have provided for us. In response to your love, we dedicate ourselves to Christ, by rejecting our selfishness, by aiming for a ministry dedicated to peace and unity among us, and all peoples.

We proclaim our desire to live by the two great commandments: To love you, and to love our neighbors. Lord, God, keep our faith strong that we may strengthen others. Let us come to

41

this table for solace and for strength, for pardon, and renewal. Send us your holy spirit, to make us one body in Christ, that we may serve the world unitedly in your name.

HYMN: Let Us Break Bread Together

COMMUNION SHARED

CELEBRANT: Risen Lord, be known to us in the breaking of bread. By him, and with him, and in him, in the unity of the Holy Spirit, all honor and glory is yours, almighty God, now and forever. Amen.

PARTICIPANTS: *THE LORD'S PRAYER*

Our Father, who art in heaven
   hallowed be thy name
Thy kingdom come, thy will be done
   on earth as it is in heaven.
Give us this day our daily bread.
   Forgive us our trespasses
   as we forgive those who trespass against us.
Lead us not into temptation
   but deliver us from evil.
For thine is the kingdom,
   and the power,
   and the glory,
Forever. Amen.

HYMN: Come, Christians, Join to Sing

BENEDICTION: The peace of God, which passes all understanding, keep your hearts and minds in the knowledge and love of God, and of Jesus Christ our Lord; and the blessing of God Almighty, the Son, and the Holy Spirit, be among you, and remain with you always. Amen.

READING NO. 3: "Wake Up, Wake Up, It's Christmas"!
A Christmas Season Sermon for the Church in Conflict

MATTHEW 1:22,23

My wife, Verna, and I have three daughters. They are grown now, but each Christmas season brings to me a flood of happy memories when they were still the little people in our house.

Christmas morning was perhaps the highlight of each year. Verna would prepare a very special breakfast. We ate with delight and haste before gathering around the tree for a Christmas song and finally to open the colorful packages.

The girls were always ecstatic to discover the packages contained the treasures of which they dreamed. Verna and I would be thrilled and happy to see their joy and excitement.

Christmas Eve was also an exciting time. In expectation of the coming morning, the girls would find it nearly impossible to go to sleep. They would stay awake far into the night, only to be sound asleep the next morning.

While Verna prepared breakfast, I would go into their bedrooms, touch them gently on the shoulder and whisper, "Wake up, wake up, it's Christmas."

The Christmas season is that time of the year when the church lightly touches the world and quietly says, "Wake up, wake up—God is with us."

MATTHEW 1:23

To Joseph the Angel announced the birth with a very proper name, Emmanuel. But when telling Mary, the Angel used a common name, Jesus.

LUKE 1:26-37

Jesus — The Son of God.
Emmanuel — God is with us.

Advent is that time of year when angels come once again to touch us gently and say, "Wake up, wake up, God is with us—and nothing is impossible with God."

To the shepherds yet another name was given, Messiah, the deliverer, the Savior. To Mary the name given was Jesus. To Joseph, Emmanuel.

Jesus — the Son of God.
Emmanuel — God is with us.
Messiah — Savior, deliverer.

My friends, these names were used to announce a gift, a gift so extravagant that all hosts of heaven wanted to join in telling it.

LUKE 2:13,14

"And on earth, peace, good will toward men."

The angels announced His birth once. But from that time on—for some 2,000 Christmases, the church has been the privileged messenger. It is the high and glorious privilege of the church in each Christmas season to gently touch the world and say, "Wake up, look up, cheer up—God is with us."

The Messiah, the deliverer, the Savior is come. And, all the world, and each one of you in it, can now have peace.

For this child, this God, this Savior, was born not only to Joseph, Mary and the shepherds, but He was born for us, A Son given to us.

ISAIAH 9:6

We have come to know Him as the Wonderful Counselor, the Mighty God, the Everlasting Father, the Prince of Peace.

"Wake up, wake up, this God is with us."

How does the church make this announcement? Certainly it tells it by its advent activities, by the ringing of the bells, the hanging of the greens, the singing of Christmas carols, by its Christmas programs and advent services.

But it also makes this announcement by its spirit of peace and its love, not only for the world, but for one another in the church, especially for one another in the church. This is how it makes the announcement all year long.

God is with us. The Prince of Peace is among us and we are meant to live together in peace and love in such a way that all who see us are moved to say, "Behold, how they love one another"! "Behold, how they pray"! "Behold, how they serve their God"!

Sadly, sorrowfully we sometimes forget that God is with us. We forget the Prince of Peace is among us.

So we become the church James is writing to when he asks, "What causes these conflicts and quarrels among you? Why do you quarrel and fight? Sinners, make your hand clean, see that your motives are pure. Be sorrowful. Mourn and weep. Turn your laughter into mourning and your gaiety into gloom. Humble yourselves before God so He might lift you high." (James 4:1-10)

What a striking contrast are His words to the singing, the joy, the gaiety which surrounds the announcement of Christ's birth.

Yes, it sometimes happens that a church forgets the Prince of Peace is among us—and that He wants all of us in the church to live in peace with one another.

Advent is a time for the church to take inventory of its internal affairs, a time to make the temple ready for the coming Messiah, the Prince of Peace.

PHILIPPIANS 2:1-11

Let us, in this grand Christmas season give our proper and fitting response to his coming among us.

Let us give glory to God in the highest and to all those around us, peace! Good will!

For God is with us. Amen.

READING NO. 4: A Devotional for a Group Which Has Resolved a Painful Conflict

HOMILY:

I am borrowing some thoughts from the words which E. Stanley Jones wrote in his little book, *Abundant Living*.

"We can thank God for pain.
Pain stabs us awake and says: 'Look out—there is something wrong here; attend to it.'
Pain is God's red flag run up to warn of danger.

But unless pain is working out to some end, it breaks us by its meaninglessness.
That is, pain can end in dull, fruitless suffering.
Or, pain can be taken up into the purposes of God and transformed into finer character,
greater tenderness and more usefulness."

Many of us have been a companion to pain for the past weeks. But each of us can choose for ourselves whether we want the pain to be fruitless or to have purpose.

We might take a little comfort from Paul's words in one of his letters to the Corinthians—they, too, were sad with pain.

SCRIPTURE: 2 Corinthians 7:8-13

HYMN: Blest Be The Tie That Binds

PRAYER:

O Loving Spirit, help us to master the pain. Fill us with your comforting spirit so that we may take hold of life when it seems impossible. Fill us with your strengthening spirit as we see the possibilities of new directions.

"Spirit of the living God, fall afresh on me. Melt me, mold me, fill me, use me.
Spirit of the living God, fall afresh on me." Amen.

READING NO. 5: A Prayer of Confession for Those Who Have Reached Agreement After a Serious Conflict

Almighty God, Father of our Lord, Jesus Christ; maker of all things; judge of all persons:
we acknowledge our many sins and the wickedness which we have committed
by thought, word, and actions against each other and against you.

We earnestly repent.
We are deeply sorry for our damaging words and our destructive behaviors;
the very memory of them causes us much grief.

Have mercy on us. have mercy on us, most merciful Father.
For thy Son, our Lord Jesus Christ's sake, forgive us all that is past;
and grant that we may ever hereafter serve thee in newness of life and unity,
to the honor and glory of thy name;
through Jesus Christ our Lord. Amen.

READING NO. 6: An Operational Model of Conflict
One way of looking at a conflict situation

INTRODUCTION

In conflict management it is essential to "sort out" the components which are operating in a particular conflict situation. You must learn to "look" at a conflict and by what you see, hear and sense, be able to answer the question: "What is the 'space' the two parties are trying to occupy at the same time, what is the 'core issue' at stake here?" Learning the components of the Operational Model will help you answer those questions.

AN OPERATIONAL MODEL OF CONFLICT

A number of components combine to make up a conflict situation; they are:

1. The TYPE of the conflict.
2. The DIMENSIONS of the conflict.
3. The TERRITORY of the conflict.
4. The BEHAVIORS intended to protect the territory.
5. The RESULTS of the conflict.

Each of these components has several different elements or dynamics, of which at least one will be present in every conflict situation. The model, next column, illustrates the relationship of the conflict components as they combine to create a conflict situation.[1]

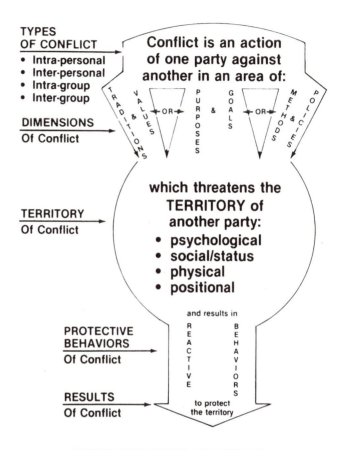

OPERATIONAL MODEL OF CONFLICT

I. Types of Conflict

There are four types or "fronts" upon which conflict may be carried out:

A. Intra-personal: Conflict within one's self, involving competing values, goals or behaviors.

B. Inter-personal: Conflict between two persons, involving certain behaviors of one which are threatening a "territory" claimed by the other.

C. Intra-group: Conflict between members of a group; a family, a congregation, a staff.

D. Inter-group: Conflict between two or more groups.

II. Dimensions of Conflict

A conflict involves one or more dimensions:

A. Values/Traditions: Deeply held, cherished principles by which a person or organization orders its life, what the person or group wants to be, to give itself to, in an ultimate sense.

This illustration is suggested by Jerry Robinson, Jr. and Roy A. Clifford, *Conflict Management in Community Groups*, University of Illinois, 1974.

B. **Goals/Purposes:** Desired future conditions that the person or organization is working to achieve.

C. **Methods/Policies:** The rules the person or group is living by and the actions taken to accomplish their goals.

III. Territories of Conflict

A. **Psychological:** "Space" within oneself; emotions, self-identity, self-esteem.

B. **Social Status:** Status within a social unit; group identity, acceptance by the group, status within a group.

C. **Physical:** Physical territory owned, occupied or claimed by a party or organization; office space, real estate.

D. **Positional:** A position of power, authority or influence occupied or claimed by a party; board chairmanship, "boss."

IV. Behaviors Intended to Protect Territory

A. **Withdraw/Divide:** To take one's territory "away" with oneself.

B. **Share/Give:** To give away some territory in order to preserve or protect the rest.

C. **Trade:** To exchange one territory for another.

D. **Take:** To take another's territory by force or influence.

E. **Withhold:** To protect one's territory by whatever means necessary.

F. **Redefine:** To draw new boundaries around one's own territory.

V. Results of Conflict

Conflict generally causes adjustments in the relationship. After confrontation (conflict in its advanced stages) things will never be exactly the same. The results may be seen in increased hostility or by increased cooperation. Following is a partial list of positive and negative results of conflict:

POSITIVE RESULTS[1]	NEGATIVE RESULTS
1. Internal dissentions and dissatisfactions are brought out into the open which enables the group to solve the problem.	1. Isolation/Division: One or more persons leave the group, or are thrown out.
2. New norms are established for more appropriate behavior.	2. Retreat: Persons are hurt and angry and "lay back" to wait for a chance to get even.
3. Goals become clear and the group is unified.	3. Disintegration: All group boundaries are destroyed and the group falls apart.
4. New energy is created for growth and productivity.	4. Sniping: The group stays together but opposing sides continue to spread rumors, carry out character assassinations.
5. Boundaries are strengthened between groups, bringing out their distinctiveness.	5. Cold War: Both sides come to fear the strength of the other and separate into isolation or "under-the-table" tactics.

[1] For a complete discussion of the functions and results of conflict in groups, see Lewis Coser, *The Functions of Social Conflict*, Glencoe, IL: The Free Press, 1971.

POSITIVE RESULTS (cont.)

6. The group is more aware of its own strength and weakness.

NEGATIVE RESULTS

6. Domination: One side realizes it is stronger than the other and seizes complete control.

CONCLUSION

Whenever you are trying to understand a conflict, ask yourself the following questions:

1. What type of conflict is this? Who are the parties involved?

2. What are the dimensions of this conflict? Over what are these persons disagreeing?

3. What is the territory being threatened? Who is feeling the threat? What is the other party doing to cause the feeling of threat? What action is the threatened party taking to protect the territory?

4. In what stage is this conflict? To what extent has mutual trust and communication eroded? Can confrontation be avoided, or is it necessary in order to "clear the air?"

READING NO. 7: Bible Study, Acts 15:1-41
A Great Conflict Chapter in the Life of the Early Church

PRIVATE STUDY:

Study the chapter prayerfully and jot down your responses to the four questions listed below. Approach the Bible study as if you had never read this Scripture before. Pray as you study, "God, what do you want to say to me through this Scripture, even now."

GROUP STUDY:

1. Allow 15 minutes private time for each person to study the chapter and jot down their responses to the four questions listed below.

2. Form groups of four-six persons to discuss their responses. Time: 30 minutes.

1. What does this Scripture tell me about God?

2. What does this Scripture tell me about human nature—even in the church?

3. What does this Scripture tell me about me? Where do I find myself in this Scripture?

4. What does this Scripture have to say about the place of conflict in my (our) ministry and church?

READING NO. 8: Analyzing the Conflict Situations in Acts 15
An Exercise for Private or Group Learning

Acts 15, the "Conflict Chapter," describes two major conflict situations in the Early Church. Please study the scriptures listed below to provide the requested information.

Conflict No.1: Acts 15:1-35

1. What stage had this conflict reached? (see vv. 1-2, 5-7)

_____

2. Define the elements of this conflict.

    A.   Type (v.v. 4-7) _____

    B.   Conflict Parties _____ vs _____

    C.   Dimensions (vv. 5,10) _____

    D.   Territory (vv. 7,9,12) _____

    E.   Behavior: Disciples:_____

Conflict No. 2: Acts 15:36-41

1. What stage did this conflict reach?

_____

2. Define the elements of this conflict.

    A.   Type _____

    B.   Conflict Parties _____ vs _____

    C.   Dimensions _____

    D.   Territory _____

    E.   Behavior_____

READING NO. 9: A Special Word for Pastors Who Are the Focus of Conflict

There are two fundamental principles for pastors who are at the center of a church conflict[1].

1. Major in Attitudes and Not in Ideology.
Make up your mind that you are going to respect *all* of the persons in the congregation. The attitude we are to have in conflict is clearly stated by Paul in Phil. 2:3-6. "Have this attitude in yourself which was also in Christ Jesus . . . Do nothing from selfishness or empty conceit, but with humility of mind let each of you regard one another as more important than himself; do not merely look out for your own personal interests, but also for the interests of others."

The pastor who has this attitude will bring peace to the conflict situation, and love to the hostile scene. The most important thing you have to bring to any church conflict is your own spirit; your attitude. The best conflict management skills in the world are secondary to this consideration; that you be a reflection of the Spirit of Christ in the midst of the conflict.

Most pastors, however, want to major in ideology. They forget that the first commandment is not about doctrinal truth but about love. In times of conflict demonstrate something of God's love for the persons engaged in the conflict and you will be amazed how issues of "correct ideology" tend to take care of themselves.

2. Major in Confrontation, not Separation.
Confront not in hostility, not through the power of your position, but in love. Meet each other, sit down and talk, listen, consult one another. Enemies will always be enemies until they talk to each other.

Finally, in order for a pastor to help a church work its way through a conflict, when he is the focus of the conflict, he must honestly face certain decisions.

a. You must decide if you really care about the people in the congregation. You must decide if you really care what's *best* for them—even if that's different from what you *want* for them.

b. You must decide if you really belong there. If you are convinced you really belong there you *never* have to defend yourself. You can then rest securely in your personal justification by

faith— which means God defends you, and you don't have to anymore.

c. You must decide whether you are really modeling Christian character and the fruits of the Spirit; love, joy, peace, gentleness, meekness, longsuffering . . . This does not mean you have to be perfect, but you do have to come back to the question, "Am I demonstrating these fruits even in the way in which I am participating in this conflict?

Phil. 4:4-9 is perhaps the greatest set of instructions Scripture has for a church leader in conflict. Never forget, these words were given as the standard of behavior in conflict, see vv. 2, 3.

THE UNIQUE NATURE OF THE CHURCH AND HOW IT RESPONDS TO CONFLICT

The congregation relates and behaves much like a family. From the very beginning of the Christian church, God has been seen as "Father," Christ as the elder "brother," we are all "brothers and sisters" in Christ. New converts are often referred to as "babes" in Christ, while elderly faithful are called "mothers" and "fathers" of the church. An established congregation may "mother" a new mission church and when two churches relate around a common purpose they are called "sister" churches.

1. The Congregation is a Family.
It can be assumed that the members are united around a core set of values. Congregations do split, members do leave—but generally only after a tremendous amount of conflict and a final conclusion that "things will *never* get better." Two assumptions can be drawn from this:

a. A congregation can generally endure a great amount of conflict without any damaging, long-range results—because the members are all searching for reasons to stay together; and,

b. in times of conflict, recalling and rehearsing the core values, the liturgy and sacraments, and the deep commitment of all the members are among our major resources for managing the conflict.

Because the congregation is a family, every conflict poses a threat to the relationships upon which is dependent for its life. Family members often tend to take even small disagreements

---

[1] From notes taken from a lecture by Rev. Arthur Brown, Baptist Church, Western Springs, IL, 1982.

more seriously than in relationships with non-family members, "If you loved me you wouldn't do that."

Almost any conflict that has progressed very far is experienced as threatening personal relationships. An interesting fall-out from this is that many pastors and leaders spend so much of their time mending relationships that they never get around to handling the actual issues which are causing the problems. And because they spend so much time mending relationships they come to believe that all conflicts in the church are "personality" conflicts — people fighting because they don't like each other, or because of a mean streak in their personality.

The truth is very few church conflicts are over personality issues. These people are family. At the core they love each other. If they didn't, it would be easy just to leave and join another congregation. yet they stay—and fight—because they do love each other and, like family, always expect every other family member to be more-or-less perfect.

Congregations tend to get into conflicts first over programs and policies (perhaps 60% of all church conflicts). Secondly, congregations tend to conflict over values and missional understandings (perhaps 25%), and finally over personality differences (perhaps 15%). However, any serious conflict left unresolved long enough will finally settle into personality differences— much like family members who cannot solve a problem eventually begin blaming each other.

2. Conflict is Generally more Threatening in Smaller Congregations than in Large.

A large congregation can generally survive a lot of conflict simply because not all the members are caught up in any one conflict. So while some are fighting, other members provide objectivity, and make sure the necessary affairs of the church are carried on in spite of the conflict.

A conflict in a small church, however, can more easily pull every one into it so that confusion reigns unchecked and everything stops while the congregation fights.

3. Conflict is Potentially More Dangerous in Certain Denominations than in Others.

For example, because the United Methodist Church values pluralism and differences of opinion, it has a great many "low grade" conflicts which sap energy from programs and mission but seldom result in church "splits." On the other hand, conservative evangelical churches place high value on unity and harmony of believers. As a result, there are fewer conflicts, but when it does occur, it is generally "high-grade" and threatens the cohesiveness of the congregation. So much so that persons often joke about church "splits" as being the main method of evangelism and church extension.

4. Even though the congregation is held together around core religious values, **effective preaching and church programming tend to generate conflicts** of value within individuals and between persons. These conflicts of values can be the means by which Christ reveals His will to individuals and congregations.

Therefore, when the church ignores or suppresses conflict, it may be hindering the work of Christ within the congregation. When pastors teach that conflict in the congregation is sinful, they may be hindering the work of the Spirit.

The type of conflict referred to here is that to which Paul referred in Romans 7:14-25. Paul experienced this conflict of values not because he was sinful (a committed sinner has no such conflict going on) but because he was responding to the call of a higher nature.

We must welcome and encourage such conflict, recognizing this conflict is because persons are coming closer to Christ, are questioning their own values and are at war within themselves. To suppress this conflict, to tell them it is because of sin, may turn them away from Christ and new life.

Freud said, "all people must try to destroy their God." They must try this to discover whether He is, in fact, their God. When the Lord came to Jacob, Jacob had to first spend the night wrestling with Him before he could receive the blessing of a new name. Had a preacher happened along and said, "Jacob, stop this sinful fighting!" He might have stopped—but he never would have known the depth of his own resistance, nor the enduring love, patience and strength of the Lord. He would not have "laid hold of the Lord." He would still have been "Jacob," and in order to make of him "Israel" the Lord would have had to allow Jacob to struggle with Him yet another time.

Spiritual Growth Resources

Dear Church Leader:

WANT TO LEARN MORE ABOUT MANAGING CHURCH CONFLICT?

This book is a companion volume to *How To Manage Conflict In The Church: Understanding and Managing Conflict.*

Volume I will give you insight into your behavior in conflict, and a three-step process of managing conflict. When you have finished your study of Volume I, you will know your preferred and back-up conflict management styles, and how to identify stages of conflict in your church.

Now that you have read volume II, you will naturally want to have volume I for your study and use in managing conflict in your own church and organization.

The two volumes may each be purchased separately, or as part of a **Conflict Management Learning System**. The Learning System also contains a cassette tape of lectures, worksheets to help gain further insight into your conflict management behavior, and a step-by-step study guide to lead you through all of the learning system materials.

I have also prepared a set of training designs for your use in training the leaders of your church to effectively manage conflict within their departments.

You will also want to know about *How to Manage Dysfunctional Conflict in the Church,* **Volume III.** It will lead you into an understanding of dysfunctional conflict situations and will give you an entirely new set of tools and approaches for working with dysfunctional persons, groups and conditions.

When the conflicts in your church seem to get worse no matter what you do, when you find yourself questioning your own leadership and counseling abilities -- the chances are you are dealing with dysfunctional conflict.

Conflicts in the church that grow out of dysfunctional relationships are different from all other types of conflict, and require entirely new tools and responses.

You may obtain all of the conflict management materials from:

SPIRITUAL GROWTH RESOURCES®

Telephone: 1•800•359•7363